Letterland

Sentence Copymasters

Sammy Snake is sitting in the sun.

Circle all Sammy Snake's letters in the sentence, then find all the things that begin with his sound.

Learn to read whole sentences

Annie Apple is in an apple tree.

Circle all Annie Apple's letters in the sentence, then find all the things that begin with her sound.

Bouncy Ben can see a big butterfly.

Circle all Bouncy Ben's letters in the sentence, then find all the things that begin with his sound.

Clever Cat can count candles.

Circle all Clever Cat's letters in the sentence, then find all the things that begin with her sound.

Dippy Duck is drawing a dog.

Circle all Dippy Duck's letters in the sentence, then find all the things that begin with her sound.

Eddy Elephant can catch every egg!

Circle all Eddy Elephants's letters in the sentence, then find the things that begin with his sound.

Firefighter Fred is feeding five fish.

Circle all Firefighter's letters in the sentence, then find all the things that begin with his sound.

Golden Girl has a very greedy goat.

Circle all Golden Girl's letters in the sentence, then find all the things that begin with her sound.

Harry Hat Man has a horse in a hat.

Circle all Harry Hat Man's letters in the sentence, then find all the things that begin with his sound.

Impy Ink is interested in insects.

Circle all Impy Ink's letters in the sentence,
then find the things that begin with his sound.

Jumping Jim can jump over jets!

Circle all Jumping Jim's letters in the sentence, then find the things that begin with his sound.

Kicking King is flying a kite.

Circle all Kicking King's letters in the sentence, then find all the things that begin with his sound.

Lucy Lamp Light loves lemons.

Circle all Lucy Lamp Light's letters in the sentence, then find all the things that begin with her sound.

Munching Mike is making a mess!

Circle all Munching Mike's letters in the sentence, then find all the things that begin with his sound.

Noisy Nick is now nine years old.

Circle all Noisy Nick's letters in the sentence, then find the things that begin with his sound.

Oscar Orange is on top of a box.

Circle all Oscar Orange's letters in the sentence, then find the things that begin with his sound.

Peter Puppy has a pretty present.

Circle all Peter Puppy's letters in the sentence, then find all the things that begin with his sound.

Quarrelsome Queen quickly makes quilts.

Circle Quarrelsome Queen's letters in the sentence, then find the things that include her sound.

Red Robot rolls to a big red rocket.

Circle all Red Robot's letters in the sentence,
then find all the things that begin with his sound.

Sammy Snake is sitting in the sun.

Circle all Sammy Snake's letters in the sentence, then find all the things that begin with his sound.

Talking Tess is talking to a tortoise.

Circle all Talking Tess's letters in the sentence, then find all the things that begin with her sound.

Uppy Umbrella goes up and up!

Circle all Uppy Umbrella's letters in the sentence, then find all the things that begin with her sound.

Vicky Violet has very nice violets.

Circle all Vicky Violet's letters in the sentence, then find the things that begin with her sound.

Walter Walrus is wet in the water.

Circle all Walter Walrus's letters in the sentence, then find all the things that begin with his sound.

Fix-it Max can see a fox in a box.

Circle all Fix-it Max's letters in the sentence, then find the things that end with his sound.

Yo-yo Man has yo-yos for sale.

Circle all Yo-yo Man's letters in the sentence, then find the things that begin with his sound.

Zig Zag Zebra zooms past the zoo.

Circle all Zig Zag Zebra's letters in the sentence, then find the things that begin with her sound.

Good day! Mr A, the Apron Man.

Circle all Mr A's letters in the sentence,
then find the things that begin with his sound.

Greetings! Mr E, the Easy Magic Man.

Circle all Mr E's letters in the sentence,
then find the things that begin with his sound.

Hi! Mr I, the Ice Cream Man.

Circle all Mr I's letters in the sentence, then find the things that begin with his sound.

Hello, Mr O, the Old Man.

Circle all Mr O's letters in the sentence,
then find the things that begin with his sound.

How do you do, Mr U, the Uniform Man.

Circle all Mr U's letters in the sentence,
then find the things that begin with his sound.